AIDS SHAMAN

Queer Spirit Awakening

by Shokti

drawing by Kairos

ISBN 978-0-244-35146-5

this book is dedicated to the angel soul known as **Woodchild**

part one HEALING IS VITAL

HIV IS THE KEY

HIV is the key
That humanity has yet to see
A key that when turned can set us free
A key that gay men urgently need to turn
There's a vital lesson to be learned
Healing Is Vital

For me HIV was the key
That revealed the spirit flowing through life
That opened the gates to eternity:
Facing mortality is the quickest way to see through life's
illusions
Befriending death the key to escaping confusion
About why we find our selves here
Why we find our selves queer
And just what is Self anyway?

Buddhists, Hindus, Pagans know
Mystical Christians Jews and Muslims know
That this is the real question to ask
But the modern world doesn't want to know
It keeps us obsessed with the trivial and inane
It prefers to medicate away all pain
Gay life doesn't want to ask the question
Of why we born this way on this rock hurtling through space
it's simpler to take more drugs
Have more sex parties

Devour more flesh
Desire more men
For some this leads to addictions and breakdowns
Has a second plague come upon our kind
But this time the sickness in the heart and mind?
In the 80s and 90s we met death up close
We learnt to face our fears
That way some of us saw there's more to the mystery of life
Than the modern world wants us to believe
Now we take pills to stem the virus
Now we can take one to prevent it getting a hold in the first
place
And we self medicate to hold off hard feelings and fears
It's so long since the dying days ended
What has happened to us in these years?

I survived the first plague
I turned the key
And now I wonder
When will gay life stop living in the shallow end
How many more casualties will there be?

HIV revealed to me...
We are born to be whole
We are born to be free
We are born to become all we can be
Beings of eternity
But we have to wake up!!!
We have really to face only one thing
Life isn't about economics, grades, muscles, money and fame
It's about playing our part in the consciousness game
We are each a part of the divine dream.

CONSIDER THIS:

HIV as a call from the soul pushing us to seek healing and understanding of who we are, to wake up as eternal spirits in the rat race of a blinkered civilisation… wake up to the discovery and formation of a bigger, brighter, braver, and much more conscious, future for gay people and all people of the Earth. Perhaps we become positive because nature and the heavens want us to take the challenge of facing and knowing ourselves, to wake up to the magnificence and potential of the soul inside, to break through the illusions of the materialist world, to break down the walls between death and life, between heaven and earth - to embrace, that at this point in our lives, for the sake of our souls, HEALING IS VITAL.

HIV was the catalyst that led to my interest in spirituality: the threat of death led me to search for meaning in life. Given a positive diagnosis in 1990, by '95 I was becoming symptomatic and was considered a PWA (Person With AIDS). I left my job, got my debts written off by telling the bank I was leaving the world, and turned my mind to the big question – why, I asked for the first time in my life, did I exist in the first place? I had held a firmly rational, materialist, atheistic view since the age of 12, but now, at 30, an understandably urgent need for spiritual answers arose in me. I plunged into a study of the worlds' religions, into pagan magic and new age teachings, soon sensing a mystical core common to all. I began to open my mind and heart to the possibility of something more, to the possibility of a purpose behind our apparently random existence here on planet earth, to the idea of a beneficent divine presence giving rise to that existence.

I had expected to be miserable about dying but instead I

became fascinated and inspired – writing, drawing, meditating, living in dreamtime for long periods, surging with energies I had never encountered before, though my experiences with lsd in gay clubs in the early 1990s had certainly prepared me for them... meeting a strong flowing, feminine, presence of divine love that I came to realise is everywhere all the time, holding us constantly, but which our mental confusion and emotional baggage – our egos - prevent us from properly knowing. I took on the notion that I was growing beyond the ego-mind and into the consciousness of the soul, starting to encounter the energy of spirit in all things. Another stage to life as a human, one that I didn't know about (but which I soon learnt has always been known in some quarters) was beginning for me. Facing death was the trigger for this journey - the journey to death's door entirely transformed my life, opening me up to a multidimensional reality in which life becomes a story of souls finding our way back home. That HOME is the internal and eternal place of connection, love, peace and glory that is our divine nature, and our divine right to realise as human beings – and facing death, overcoming fear of dying, is a fast track way to get there, one that was offered to the gay community so early in our story of political and social liberation – to accelerate our growth on so many levels, personal and collective.

HIV pushed me to the point of asking the most important question there is, and it was a catalyst for a rapid spiritual awakening – for an Accelerated Individual Discovery of Self. By surrendering to the prospect of annihilation I experienced Self beyond the limits of my individuality. This place beyond ego is what many experience through sacred medicine, such as Ayahuasca, but any good spiritual practice or ritual takes us beyond identification with the little self into discovery of the greater Self, revealing just how much more to our existence, to our consciousness, there really is. Facing death opened the doors of perception for me, showing me that as a queer man my entire being surges with raw, creative energy of spirit, and that whatever some religions might say, we queers have a relationship with the spirit worlds that is central to who we are.

DANCE ON TOWARDS A NEW EARTH

Calling to The Radical Wayfarers
That come from the Root
Inventing new dreams and new schemes
This is our time to
Assemble, Coalesce
Dance on towards
A New Earth.

Calling to the Peaceful People
All around the world
Who no longer wish to tolerate
This theatre of the absurd
Assemble, Coalesce
We dance on towards
A New Earth.

Calling to the Believers in Love
Who need no church and no creed
Who have had enough
Of the corruption and greed
We dance on towards
A New Earth.

The Awakening Children
Of the Mother Divine
Rising to our calling
This is the Time
For the return of the Goddess
And the end of Men's Madness
The old ways remembered

The cycles once more honoured
A mystery unveiling
For those with eyes to see
The calling to love
The calling to be free
Lovers, Peacemakers, Radical Wayfarers
Assemble, Coalesce
We dance on towards a New Earth.

"Out of the mists of our long oppression,
We bring love for ourselves and each other,
And love for the gifts we bear,
So heavy and so painful the fashioning of them,
So long the road given us to travel them. A separate people,
We bring a gift to celebrate each other,
'Tis a gift to be gay!
Feel the pride of it!"

"We have been a SEPARATE PEOPLE…. Drifting together in a parallel existence, not always conscious of each other.. yet recognising one another by eyelock when we did meet… here and there as outcasts… Spirit people… in service to the Great Mother.. Shamans.. mimes and rhapsodes, poets and playwrights, healers and nurturers… VISIONARIES… REBELS"

"Our beautiful lovely sexuality is the gateway to spirit. Under all organised religions of the past, Judaism, Christianity, Islam, there has been a separation of carnality, or shall we say of flesh or earth or sex, and spirituality. As far as I am concerned they are all the same thing, and what we need to do as faeries is to tie it all back together again."

Harry Hay, 1912-2002, **gay rights activist and radical faerie founding father**

THE GAY BOYS ALL LEFT FOR THE CITY

The gay boys all left for the city
Leaving no-one who sings to the trees
The gay boys all left for the city
And got trapped by desire and disease.
They went to seek out love and sex
But they forgot their other needs.

The gay boys all left the village
And left the wisdom of seasons behind
They chase after constant pleasures
So happy to have found their kind
They chase after so much ecstasy
They believe they are living free
But when we forget the cycles of nature
Mind and body succumb to disease.

The gay boys all left for the city
To get high as the sun and the breeze
But the gay boys became good capitalists
And got caught by desire and disease.

THE GODDESS AND PAN

We queers are children of the Goddess and Pan
We don't answer to the angry God made by man
Our god didn't die on a cross
And those of us in the know
know the Great Mother is the real boss.
We have always been her servants and lovers
In Temples, Forests and Fields
We are Faeries Fools and Tricksters
Shaman Brothers and Witch Sisters
We've been hiding until the men forgot
Why they'd banished us in the first place
and we're still here where we always were
We're Here, we're Queer, we're Cosmic.

So here's our next steps
Its time to regain access to
The cosmic power of Lesbos
The magical gifts of the Benders
The forgotten powers of the Transgendered
Be Here Be Queer Be Cosmic
Precious to humanity are we
Reclaim the ancient ways
Renew them for today
Sexuality is a sacred gift
Designed for sharing with each other
Love is what makes us human and divine
In us lie the keys to enter heaven's rhyme
The Rainbow rises, this is the time.

Ancestor voices left their messsages for us to find....

"Divine am I inside and out, and I make holy whatever I touch or am touch'd from, The scent of these armpits is aroma finer than prayer, This head more than churches, bibles and all the creeds... if I worship one thing more than another it shall be the spread of my own body"

"I celebrate myself, and sing myself,
And what I assume you shall assume,
For every atom belonging to me as good belongs to you."

"And as to you death, and you bitter hug of mortality.. it is idle to try to alarm me......
And as to you corpse, i think you are good manure, but that does not offend me.....
And as to you life, i reckon you are the leavings of many deaths,
No doubt i have died myself ten thousand times before.
I hear you whispering there O stars of heaven....."

Walt Whitman 1819-1892

"we are arriving at one of the most fruitful and important turning points in the history of the race. the Self is entering into relation with the Body. for, that the individual should conceive and know himself, not a toy and a chance-product of his own bodily heredity, but as identified and continuous with the Eternal Self of which his body is a manifestation, is indeed to begin a new life and to enter a hitherto undreamed world of possibilities....this transformation, whilst the greatest and most wonderful, is also of course the most difficult in Man's evolution, for him to effect. it may roughly be said that the whole of the civilisation-period in Man's history is the preparation for it."

"When the individual self, reaching union with the universal, becomes consciously and willingly the creator and inspirer of the body – that is indeed a Transfiguration. The individual is no longer under the domination of the body and its heredity, but rising out of this tomb becomes lord and master of the body's powers, and identified with the immortal Self of the world."

"I say that I think perhaps of all the services the Uranian may render to society it will be found some day that in this direction of solving the problems of affection and of the heart he will do the greatest service. If the day is coming as we have suggested – when Love is at last to take its rightful place as the binding and directing force of society (instead of the Cash-nexus), and society is to be transmuted in consequence to a higher form, then undoubtedly the superior types of Uranians – prepared for this service by long experience and devotion, as well as by much suffering – will have an important part to play in the transformation. For that the Urnings in their own lives put Love before everything else – postponing to it the other motives

like money-making, business success, fame, which occupy so much space in most people's careers – is a fact which is patent to everyone who knows them. This may be saying little or nothing in favour of those of this class whose conception of love is only a poor and frivolous sort; but in the case of those others who see the god in his true light, the fact that they serve him in singleness of heart and so unremittingly raises them at once into the position of the natural leaders of mankind."

Edward Carpenter 1844-1929

LSD, BUTTERFLIES AND STARLIGHT

god was in the microdots
when i was a gay caterpillar:
she opened my mind, showed me lots
but it was only later i joined the dots
when HIV forced to me to retreat and face mortality.

humans are caterpillars
eating up the goodness of life on earth
when our consumption is out of control
sooner or later a crisis
will force us to pupate and enter rebirth.
life is an archetypal journey
in fact many such journeys overlapping
not a random chance, not an idiot's dance
this is the game of awakening we are playing.

do you know that you are starlight?
focussed into a human body?
o THEY told you you are stardust
and to dust you shall return
but that's because there's a secret to life
THEY don't want you to learn.
That's that we're all BUTTERFLIES
bringing colour to the world
from egg to larva to chrysalis to imago
there are four stages through which to grow
most humans are still at the caterpillar stage
little do they know
of the universe of the butterfly

where life is lived with wings in flight
and seen in psychedelic golden light.
HIV was my cocoon, i wove myself in
and prepared to die, while doing so
opening my mind to the sky
the light shone in and transformation began
evolving from caterpillar to butterfly man.
Learn to fly queer brothers!
Don't wait for disaster to find your wings
But remember too Icarus
Keep a grip on reality, don't fly too high
We are explorers of consciousness
and the ship is our sanity.
We are emissaries of love
come to break the rules and teach the fools
there's more to life than money and power
everyone has a soul that needs nurture and care
everyone is a soul that seeks to become AWARE

"I am conscious.. that behind all this artistic beauty.. there is some spirit hidden of which the painted forms and shapes are but modes of manifestation, and it is with this spirit that I desire to become in harmony.... We have forgotten that water can cleanse, and fire purify, and the earth is Mother to us all... I feel sure that in elemental forces there is purification, and I want to go back to them and live in their presence..."

"It will be a marvellous thing – the true personality of man – when we see it. It will grow naturally and simply, flowerlike, or as a tree grows. It will not be at discord. It will never argue or dispute. It will not prove things. It will know everything. And yet it will not busy itself about knowledge. It will have wisdom. Its value will not be measured by material things..... "'Know thyself' was written over the portal of the antique world. Over the portal of the new world, 'Be thyself' shall be written."

Oscar Wilde 1854-1900

RETURN OF THE SHAMANS

and the time must come
after all the parties
all the drugs
after the dying years
and a decade of decadence
the time comes, can only come
when the gay phoenix rises
after centuries of death
across the planet
the rainbow serpent
unicorn lion and bear
the return of the shamans
awakening everywhere
in every culture, every race and faith
rainbow children awakening
to the power and the light
liberation of the spirit
free to be ourselves
queer magic calls us to our wealth
earth are we
fire are we
air are we
water are we
beyond gods and without creed
we fulfil a fundamental need
opening the gates as we find our place
the shamans of the human race
the world is lost in delusions
of fame, glamour, money and hate
since the men of war closed the faerie gate

shut out the magic, stamped down the female
spiritually castrated the men who love men
war and commerce dominate the globe
the great mother was disrobed
and pain strangles life to death
faerie men seek within
find the place where it all begins
be reborn in the dragon's flames
move on from stupid attitude games
in this journey we are all the same
vulnerable, strong, we're each part of the song
the world will awaken when we become one
brothersisterhood
finding where we belong
singing the shaman's song
the time must come
after all the parties
all the drugs
after the dying years
and a decade of decadence
the time comes, can only come
when the gay phoenix rises
after centuries of death
across the planet
the rainbow serpent
unicorn lion and bear
the return of the shamans
awakening everywhere
if we don't wake up and claim our inheritance
from the tribal ancestor spirits
our kind will be repressed again
across the world our future is in the balance
this flowering has been attempted before

"We're the people who bring the beauty into the world and actually create the culture... We're the people who make Spirit move, and the world is so much richer for it."

Clyde Hall, Shoshone tribe, ceremonial leader of the Dance for All Peoples

"All began in love, all seeks to return in love. Love is the law, the teacher of wisdom, and the great revealer of mysteries."

"Let there be beauty and strength, power and compassion, honor and humility, mirth and reverence within you."

"The Goddess falls in love with Herself, drawing forth her own emanation, which takes on a life of its own. Love of self for self is the creative force of the universe. Desire is the primal energy, and that energy is erotic: the attraction of lover to beloved, of planet to star, the lust of electron for proton. Love is the glue that holds the world together."

Starhawk, Witch and Teacher

part two ACCELERATED INDIVIDUAL DISCOVERY OF SELF

THE SPIRIT AND THE FLESH

the spirit and the flesh
the body is the power
ecstasy is the glory
it doesn't matter the details of your consensual sexual story
it does matter how we do it
which frequencies we share
it matters whether we love each other
we got a choice to be demons or brothers
we got the choice to care
we got the chance to be aware
take me to ecstasy
open body, heart and mind
soar into connection
and escape the daily grindrrrrr
let's find the way to reach the light
because men are born to love not fight
and tell the world it can be free
from fear and hate and stupidity
when love rules the subtle waves of consciousness
humanity will rise above it's unrest
and life be seen as the eternal quest
of the One in the All and the All as One
the Queer Age of Aquarius has begun.

guys! Our consciousness is vast
goes way beyond the skies

we are consciousness explorers
we came to evolve fast
that's why we chase the highs
sex and drugs shift reality
take us to the edges of sanity
to discover the extremes the body can take
to realise the joys our souls can make
riding high on the pleasure connection
we are love incarnate, with a brain, heart and dick
seems we have to balance it all
seems too much pleasure makes u sick
we got 7 chakras to expand
sex is only part of who we are, we are not homo-sexual
we are homo-sapiens too
what happens when we marry the two?
EVOLUTION. Life is speeding up, higher selves are now on
line
we are entering multidimensional time
it's easier with an open heart
but it's coming anyway, life's in deep transition
and I offer this perspective from the visionary position:
queers we hold a key to these times
we open the gateways to the higher mind
when we open our sex and love centres
we really are space and time benders
the world has forgotten what we holy children do
and those amongst us who remember it….. are few.
Yet it is the core of me and you
and somewhere on the dance floor
or via powders and pipes
I know you have felt it
and known this is true.

When I meet a man to touch and kiss
open the channels that lead us to bliss
I wanna step outside of mind and into sensation
our love making an act of spiritual creation
surrender to pleasure go deep in each moment
loving the self that is love itself
the power, the light, the source of the soul
glory and victory, sex to be whole
love and awareness the true and ultimate goal.

"To be gay is something that begins within ourselves. In begins in our hearts, in that place that is never separate from the living heart of Infinite Oneness. To be gay is something that begins with ourselves, that finds itself mirrored back, echoed back to us by the tribe of men who love men. This tribe, our people , is a scouting tribe, a Walks-Between people, bridge-making people, walking between men and women, between night and day, between matter and spirit, between the living and the dead."

"When purposeful, spiritual connection is forgotten, the depth of sexual connection often takes it place. Sex points one in the right direction, deep into the self, into the mystery. But sex alone is not the answer to the gay dilemma of the present, the sense of meaninglessness. A sense of spiritual participation in the community of the planet is the answer. For no one else will tell us our purpose. Its discovery must come from ourselves."

"We enter a new era in our history. We enter an era when love and not pain will be our teacher, when joy and not sorrow will colour our lives. Never before on this planet have people lived this way. But after thousands and thousands of years of struggle and growth, we have come to the point in time when all of us fill be fully incarnate in our bodies, fully present as spirits manifesting in physical form. Without our wisdom and our power, humanity cannot make it to the next cycle. With our power and wisdom, shared freely with the tribe of all tribes, everything is possible"

Andrew Ramer, Two Flutes Playing (1997)

QUEER SHAMANS

play, dance and work in light and dark
not afraid of either
for they are in touch with the ether
and the rainbow that lies beyond
the illusion of duality
the effects of electromagnetism and gravity
they've come to restore some sanity
QUEER SPIRIT
calls together awakening queers in touch with nature and
spirit…
… explorers of consciousness, lust and love…
of laughter, light and liberation
The potential lies in us to bring together day and night
To reveal the multiverse beyond
To sing the Goddess song.
Sometimes that song is full of rage
Sometimes it's sweet and nurturing
Unlocking the gifts of crone and sage
The next chapter of the Aquarian story

Calling to the Witch in every Queer
To the Priestess in every Lesbian
To the Shaman in every Gay barman
The Divine Mother in every Bear
The Abbot in every Faggot
The Deity in every Dyke
The Radical in every Faerie
It's time for the **QUEER PEOPLES OF PLANET EARTH
TO COME HOME**

"The position that gay people take in society, the function we so often choose, is that of mediator between worlds..... In a tribal environment, this means shape shifting into wolves, birds, stones, wind and translating their wisdoms for the benefit of the people of the tribe... in the long patriarchal history that has gradually enveloped the world's people, the gay function has been to make crossover journeys between gender-worlds, translating, identifying and bringing back the information ....gay culture is always on the cusp of each intersecting world or way of life, on the path between one world and another."

"The tribal attitude said, and continues to say, that Gay people are especially empowered because we are able to identify with both sexes and can see into more than one world at once, having the capacity to see from more than one point of view at a time."

Judith Grahn, Another Mother Tongue
1984

ONE SPIRIT

One Spirit seeks to know itself through its infinite creation
One Spirit seeks to feel itself and know its own elation
So it gives itself to everything
It becomes the Many and the One
Evolving through the aeons
Until its tale is done.
To us it gives the sense of Self
of individuality, intellect and empathy
so we can ask Who Am I?
Unlike the rock or bear or baby –
we can seek inside ourselves for answers
and thus complete the tale,
if we can face the challenge
of dropping the little ego and embracing the real Self
We are the One Light and Love and Life
and so is everybody else.
If the simplicity of reality became apparent today
would anybody believe life could be so gay?
I am You, You are Me, we are in a fantasy
a condensed reality designed to set us free
we've been told to believe we are individuals
but that is so far from the truth
we are all part of the connected matrix of consciousness
the One Spirit on the loose
as we wake up one by one to the miracle and mystery
an end to the journey through darkness is in sight
we approach the start of a new one.... in the Light
of ONE SPIRIT

"If I go into the place in myself that is love, and you go into the place in yourself that is love, we are together in love. Then you and I are truly in love, the state of being love. That's the entrance to Oneness."

"Souls love. That's what souls do. Egos don't, but souls do. Become a soul, look around, and you'll be amazed-all the beings around you are souls. Be one, see one. When many people have this heart connection, then we will know that we are all one, we human beings all over the planet. We will be one. One love. And don't leave out the animals, and trees, and clouds, and galaxies-it's all one. It's one energy."

"The spiritual journey is not about acquiring something outside yourself, rather, you are penetrating deep layers and veils to return to the deepest truth of your own being."

"The universe is made up of experiences that are designed to burn out your attachment, your clinging, to pleasure, to pain, to fear, to all of it. And as long as there is a place where you're vulnerable, the universe will find a way to confront you with it."

"The point isn't to deny our Egos, but to extricate ourselves from our exclusive preoccupation with them."

RAM DASS, Spiritual Teacher

BE HERE BE QUEER BE COSMIC

Wake Up to a new Reality, the true nature of Duality
we Exist in our Fullness, Individual You and Me
but at the Core we are Oneness
it's not so hard to see
we love to shift to Altered Realities
when we make JOY our goal
we make way for the Soul
to take over the reins for a while
we surrender to the journey
mind dropped we find release
we go into our Spirit
the mental torture cease
the mind thinks we are separate
so it fucks us over every time
but the Heart leads us to Connection
Love brings us into Rhyme
then life becomes a Dance
we wake up from the trance
the Rainbow Age is coming
so learn to quell the mind
and see what you will find
the Gateways to Bliss exist right there
we just switch them on inside
if we can relinquish pride
and fear from the agenda
we open the way to switch on
the magical gifts of the Benders
the forgotten power of the Transgendered
be here be queer be cosmic
precious to humanity are we

be Here be Queer be Cosmic
we are souls born to be free
but unless we take the journey to know the Self
our inner eyes won't open, we won't be able to see
the miracle all around us
and the destiny for faggotry
SEXUALITY is a sacred gift
a soul can give another
so much treasure in that merging
when we treat each other as brother
SO MUCH SADNESS when we don't
when our games become just bullshit
LOVE is what makes us human and divine
CHOOSE IT and enter the Rhyme
the Rainbow rises and soon comes its time.

We forgot how to live in the dreamtime
Now we only dream when asleep
We no longer fly with the rainbow spirits and faerie elementals
We are herded through life like sheep
But the rainbow spirits and faerie elementals
Are still right here alongside us
Waiting for our sleep to end
And our magic eyes to re-open
In a world full of spirit, in a queer universe
Queer Spirit calls us, to remember, to play, to laugh
To love, to shine, to serve.
Be Here Be Queer Be Cosmic

HIV POINTS US TO THE HEART OF THE MATTER

HIV points us to the heart of the matter
a virus calling us to heal in body, mind and soul.
Healing is Vital, even a virus plays a role
on our human journey to becoming whole.
who are we? what do we want in our lives?
in what ways can we care for ourselves better?
HIV will make us ask these things
we might learn that our answers, our thinking affects how we feel
we might see that emotional well-being leads to physical health
we might see what is false and what is real
in our lives as we grope forwards in the darkness
not knowing if sickness lurks down the line
not knowing if we're living on borrowed time
at the same time we're liberated from fear of infection
bareback sex offers itself from every direction
chem fuelled party life that brings escape from the anguish
and a sense both of brotherhood and release
our unspoken truth that since we are infected and life may be short
we may as well live it to the high vibrational max
glory in our bodies, our shamanic rituals
and the joy we can give or take from each other
whether we are long term or momentary lovers.
It's hard to be motivated to work for the system
or try to improve life on earth
when you don't see the point any more
you've been told all your life your existence is abhorrent
perhaps you started to believe it?

Society would like us to take the pills and continue to feed the
economic dream
but HIV wants to teach us that life is more than it seems
wants us to face our demons, heal our wounds and discover our
potential
for the sake of those to come, our success is essential.
If we just take the pills and don't take the healing journey
we are missing the light within the darkness
and the darkness will eventually swallow us up.
here's the rub:
HIV is the middle name of GOD
SHIVA SHIVA SHIVA SHIVA
the dancer, the destroyer, the oneness sublime
calling calling to the people of earth
to find his divine presence **INSIDE**
All life's crises hold an opportunity
nothing is ever only dark or light
HIV can awaken our spiritual sight.
Gays don't like religion, thank goddess for that
we prefer to think for ourselves
and that's where it's at
we come out because we touch the truth inside
and that's where we find our love and our pride
if we learn to listen to the soul, as we did as a child
all the answers we seek are there.
we are not just biology, chemistry, physics
we are mind, emotion and ecstatic spirit
we are air, water, earth and fire
HIV is not the end, it's a stepladder to a life lived higher
drugs are a shortcut, or a signpost on the way
whether they become our master or we master them
we will have to move on from them one day
once we've opened our energy bodies through all that play

we come back to **CONSCIOUSNESS** as the only WAY.
We can break through all pain and fear
discover there's so much more to being queer
we're called gay because our souls were born happy
unconditional engagement with life lived from the heart
we brighten the world when we fulfil our art
of enchantment, love and play
HIV can take us to the heart of the matter
the heart of being gay.

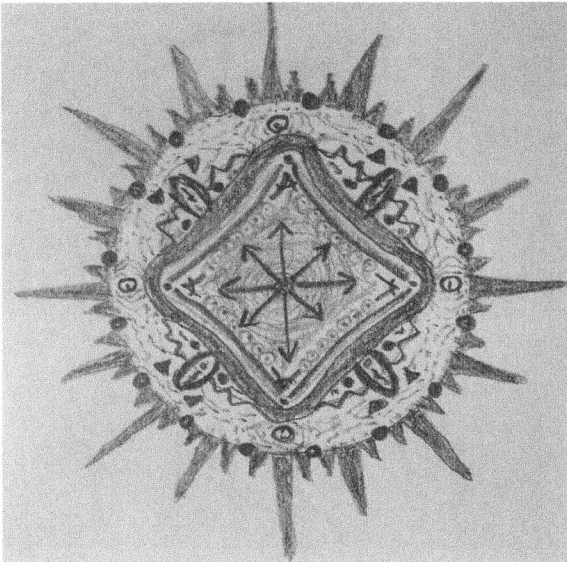

"What if we smashed the mirrors
And saw our true face?
What if we left the Sacred Books to the worms
And found our True Mind?
What if we burned the wooden Buddhas?
Gave the stone Buddhas back to the mountains?
Dispersed the gurus with a great laugh
And discovered the path we had always been on?"

Elsa Gidlow 1898-1986

QUEER MYSTIC

queer mystic knows life and death as ONE
is prepared to work hard for the Source
but it has to be FUN
he wants all to consider themselves
as sons of the moon and daughters of the SUN
we are children born to love and pray
we get to know ourselves this way.

take the sacred out of life
and we lose the rudder, the wheel, the light
adrift on lonely planet earth
we forget that we are here to serve
Mother Nature
and not the reverse.

Gathering in circle our spirits lift and connect
like a flock, a herd or shoal
we learn to move as ONE BEING
both separate and ONE WHOLE.

Gathering from the heart
we simply discover our art
keeping earth and sky in play
we celebrate the brand new WAY
UNVEIL THE ROLE QUEER BEINGS HAVE
IN BIRTHING THIS NEW DAY.

combining genders, linking worlds
sacred love forever unfurled.

GOD IS ALIVE, GOD IS WITHIN
GODDESS IS ALIVE, GODDESS IN EVERYTHING
MAGIC IS ALIVE, MAGIC COMES FROM WITHIN
MAGIC IS AFOOT, AFOOT IN EVERYTHING

Eyannis

"For things are changing. The voices of the gods have fallen silent. They no longer speak from heaven above—that turned out to be only sky. The gods now speak in our human voices. It is in human consciousness that the divine now manifests itself to itself. And our gay consciousness, we can discover, potentially now speaks to us— and through us to the whole human race—that secret message that lies at the core of religion.

"Gay people are bellwethers, early adopters, leading indicators; as well the "canaries-in-the-mine," poised on the cutting (bleeding?) edge of evolution. Whether we know it or not—or call ourselves gay or not—our lives and struggles change the world. And there's still more changing to do.

"I'm not trying to create a theory or system but to articulate, as forthrightly as I can, what is already obvious to us as gay. It's a gay thing, after all, to want to be the little boy who shouts the truth that no one else dares admit: The Emperor's new clothes are a hoax and don't actually exist! (Though it is also a gay thing to have devised the hoax and tricked the Emperor by his own pretensions into walking naked through the downtown streets.) That's what we understand about many of the beliefs "normal people" take for granted. Our ability to dis-identify with collective delusion constitutes a true spiritual path, one born of our homosexual experience. Yet nothing about the benefits of a gay spiritual path invalidates or diminishes the non-gay path; we're not in competition with them. We just have our own path. And every sincere path benefits every other sincere path. Homosexuality is not automatically a spiritual path to enlightenment (one of the grouses routinely directed against the gay spiritual movement). But if you're homosexual and you want to get enlightened or you want to be a saint, then

your homosexuality must be part of your getting there."
Toby Johnson, author **Gay Spirituality and Gay Perspective**

THE RAINBOW PEOPLE

We are the rainbow people
we appear in every race and nation
we are people of love and joy
we are not our sexuality
we are the ones who bring peace
tolerance and colour
we are passion and liberation
found through pain and pleasure
we are the rainbow people
love joy and liberation
is the mission of our nation
some of us are gay
some lesbian, bisexual or transgendered
but it's our hearts and minds as well as our sex
that makes us who we are
we are both male and female
made of flesh and spirit
connecting worlds is our calling
now comes the time for us to live it
yet most of us seem blind
to the spirit that we are
so many lies are told about us
so many seem to hate us
we haven't found our own worth yet
haven't unlocked all our treasures
is it any wonder
we get so hooked on pleasures?

In our lusts and in our passions
burns the fire of life

in our open minds and unfurling love
lies the way to light
light of many colours
rainbows shall fill the void
we are channels, vessels and lightbeams
born to show there is more to life
here to reveal and paint the rainbow
peace, love and understanding for everyone
children of moon and sun
rainbow warriors, multidimensional
sexy souls simply sensational
love joy and liberation

Don't define us by our sex
don't define us by our gender
know us by our hearts
by our transcendent arts

A global upsurge of difference
a love that dares to speak its name
that demands the end of fear and shame
it's time to play a cosmic game.

We've been hidden for so long
in every race on earth
waiting for the globe to shrink
so we can find each other
pathological said the shrinks
sinners said the church
we have to fight for equality
and in ourselves we have to search
for the answers to why we we're here
for the secrets of being Queer.

This is the calling of the twenty first century queer:
to learn to unite the sexual and the spiritual
and find the balancing, healing, role we play in the human
family
to remember, recover and renew our **QUEER SPIRIT**

"We look forward to creating a genuine Gay culture, one that is free from exploitation by bars, baths, and gay business owners. We look forward to re-establishing women's mysteries and men's mysteries as the highest expression of collective Gay culture and sexuality. We look forward to regaining our ancient historical roles as medicine people, healers, prophets, shamans and sorcerers. We look forward to an endless and fathomless process of coming out – as gay people, as animals, as humans, as mysterious and powerful spirits that move through the life cycle of the cosmos..... Like butterflies we are emerging from the shells of our past restricted existence. We are re-discovering the ancient magic that was once the birth right of all human beings. We are re-learning how to talk to the worms and the stars. We are taking flight on the wings of self-determination. Come, blessed Lady of the Flowers, Queen of Heaven, creator and destroyer, Kali – we are dancing the dance of your coming."

Arthur Evans, Witchcraft and the Gay Counter-Culture

NO SEPARATION

'This is to be understood by the heart, there is no separateness at all.' Upanishads

sages have always appeared on this earth
to tell us we are more than a physical birth
the kingdom of consciousness lies within
when we know this an age of love will begin

quantum physics tells us matter is an illusion
inside the atom there is mainly space
we desperately need to break out of confusion
and move forwards the story of the human race

religions scream at and fight each other
while many deny spirit all together
when will we see all as sister and brother
and embrace the fact that we exist FOREVER

you are not that personality
you are not that body or mind
get over the effects of gravity
and open to what's there to find

the body is the temple of the soul
and the brain the receiver that lets consciousness in
if we open to spirit we have the chance to be whole
and a new age on earth can begin

I am You, You are I
we are one being on the way

no more separation
this is the day

the mystery of enlightenment
the promise of salvation
secrets are out in the open
there is no separation.

we must reconnect to the miracle
find the seat of awe inside
if we cannot see the wonder
something in the soul has died

it's a miracle we are here
on this rock in space called earth
it's a miracle that the queer
are now free to find our worth

we have been hated for an age or two
though we have also had our flowerings
now is the moment of our greatest liberation
what are we doing with it?

If we use each other like commodities
and neglect to engage the heart
we will suffer addiction and disease
our lives gradually fall apart

we seem to have forgotten
we are children of nature and the stars
we badly need to wake up to the miracle
and heal our weeping scars

queers are born to a quest
to search for self, for love and health
we are at our best
when in the soul we find our wealth

"Some call the Creator of this Universe God, but our earliest ancestors, when they looked in awe at the world around them and tried to understand where it came from, saw the ultimate creative force as Goddess, as Mother. The Father of our culture created the world by speaking it into existence. The Mother of our ancestors birthed the universe from her body. There was no separation between Creator and creation. And as we shift our thinking and come back to this ancient wisdom, we will find balance and healing for ourselves. Ultimately the Creator is neither male nor female, but Oneness. It is the Prime Vibration. It is Absolute Information. In Seeing It as Mother we honour own own capacity for connection, compassion, clarity and communion of the soul. In knowing It as Mother we cycle back to the beginning of this era so that we can step into the next in wholeness.

"The liturgies of the Father are spoken, as revelation comes the from the Father in words, for with words he created the universe. The universe itself is the revelation of the Mother, and her liturgies are of the body. As we open to seeing her and her creation, as we learn to feel our place in it and know that we are never separate from it, and cannot ever be separate from it, then everything we becomes a prayer. Anchored in love, our bodies filled with joy, reaching out in ecstasy to express our gratitude, we ground the Mother's bliss in the world.

"In our Mother's world we do not have to struggle for enlightenment, Her light is always with us. We do not have to be reborn, for each moment of our lives is a new creation in her infinite, eternal body, and we are always a part of it."

Andrew Ramer, Two Flutes Playing

THOUGH HEARTS MAY HURT AND SOMETIMES BREAK THERE IS ALWAYS MORE LOVE TO MAKE

Death came to get me
the doctor said
in seven years you are surely dead

Death crept around
and brought decay
but my life was not about to end that way
open wide open high
surrender to earth, rise into sky
death showed me there was more to life
more to me than the mind bound I.

Led by the goddess on a path of love
where all things are one and there is always enough
taught to be satisfied by the prospect of death
and shown that infinity is reached thru the breath
I dropped who I was and became who I am
an infinitely expanding yet still quite small man
who seeks nothing more than to bring love, to bring light
help my sisters and brothers see through the night
to each that comes I open my heart
even though maybe one day we'll part
nothing is permanent though love is the key
through opening and opening we all come to see
that though hearts may hurt and sometimes break
there is always more love to make
though we might seem to get lost up the path
it's ourselves we are finding, together or apart

"Holy! Holy! Holy! Holy! Holy! Holy! Holy! Holy! Holy!
Holy! Holy! Holy! Holy! Holy! Holy!
"The world is holy! The soul is holy! The skin is holy! The nose
is holy! The tongue and cock and hand and asshole holy!
Everything is holy! everybody's holy! everywhere is holy!
everyday is in eternity! Everyman's an angel!
The bum's as holy as the seraphim! the madman is holy as you
my soul are holy!...
Holy the sea holy the desert holy the railroad holy the
locomotive holy the visions holy the hallucinations holy the
miracles holy the eyeball holy the abyss!
Holy forgiveness! mercy! charity! faith! Holy! Ours! bodies!
suffering! magnanimity!
Holy the supernatural extra brilliant intelligent kindness of
the soul!"

Allen Ginsbery, from Howl. 1926-1997

AGE OF AQUARIUS

This is the morning of the Age of Aquarius
Breakfast has been prepared
Light Love and Laughter are on the table
But humanity is running scared
The world has become very unstable
So few are enjoying the Aquarian feast
Only a few are able.
Folks are running around, still locked in a dark dream
Not realising life is so much more than it once seemed
Locked in dark dreams of power, fear and fame
Unaware we could be living a different game
A game of remembering, discovering, awakening
To a quantum reality of love
Souls coming home in age of war and corruption
The Aquarian birth will be an eruption
And everything we know will change.

So let's start the feast
Break the fast of Unknowing
Feed on Light, soak up Love
And accept that we're growing
Into a single conscious human family
Released from millennia of insanity.

This is the morning of the Age of Aquarius
Since the dawn things got quite chaotic
But when the crying's done and the day begun
Life's gonna get more erotic
When we unlock the sacred secrets of sexuality
Life's gonna be more liberated and exotic.

When we get over the fear and shame about sex
And celebrate the holy gift that it is
When society ceases the war on drugs
And embraces the shamans in its midst
The royal journey to Consciousness will proceed
The sunrise of the Age of Aquarius
Queers sowing the seeds.

Seeds of life
Seeds of light
Seeds of love
Dispelling the night

How many are now waking up
To the reality that life is one dance
One system, one expression
Of the infinite in the infinitesimal
Of the breath of creation made flesh
Of a love divine that transcends the mind
More than flesh
More than ego
The soul inside is who we are
There is glory in our flesh
And eternity in our hearts
We are earth, wind, water and fire
Our souls are ever calling us higher
To a new paradigm
Where we sense the connections
And where we express our passions
Our ideas and affections
Where conflicts resolve
And we rapidly evolve

Into mastery and light
Dimensions collide
Rebirth from the inside
OUT

I am Shokti Lovestar, poet and ritual celebrant
My calling is to serve the evolution, the awakening
Of the divine potential in human consciousness
By honouring the seasons, the moons, the sun, the elements
I co-create rituals that open, uplift and heal the soul
Creating community of beings connected through the 4th and 5th
dimensions
Re-enchanting the world.

THINGS GAY BOYS FORGET

Things gay boys forget
phallic worship is an ancient holy rite
through the rising cock we raise the male god energy
we can be empowered by this, in body heart and mind
the god energy is sacred, we his sacred manifestation
which is why we need to treat each other as brothers
brothers on a sacred path called life, a mystery in deeds
not pieces of meat or strangers to meet and greet with greed
with whom we desperately must exchange seed
the pagan worlds all celebrated sexuality as a divine sacrament
the patriarchal religions made sex a dark taboo, a restricted rite
they cut people off from the power sex opens up in us
power transcendence bliss and insight
now we are free to be sexual as never before
with internet, backrooms, saunas and scruff
with poppers and uppers, blue pills and stuff
til we find out if its possible to ever have enough
we know we are flesh, we know our desires
but we are not sure any more if we have souls
science and hatred of religion have squeezed them out of our
vocabulary
we believe we live only once, so we feel in such a rush
and we pretend we can rule life from the mind
and run wild with the desires
never mind what we might find
and if we have souls
then the whole thing is wrong
we are not evil, love is our song
and we do have souls, hearts that shine
spirits that fly and fall sometimes

bodies that crave attention
and the wounded child should get a mention
we broke out of the sexuality taboo
we could break the spiritual barrier too
life exists beyond our senses
and we are much more than what we find here
we havent been around the block, survived a plague
and partied like it's the end of all time
and not learnt a thing or two
we are much more than what we find here
we are sacred, we are queer
beyond labels, beyond fear
life is sacred, life is queer
there need be no more blocks to love here
aquarius is here, aquarius is queer

"It's important to realize that you have the divine on your side, that the divine is not against love, or the body or sexuality, the divine wants the complete flowering of body, heart, mind and soul together to produce a completely different kind of human being. This is what Walt Whitman saw. Whitman is the supreme prophet poet of the last three hundred years. The one who really understood the deepest possible connections between sexual liberation and the birth of democracy and the freedom of all beings to live their complete lives in the sanctification of nature. If gay people really read Whitman's poems, they'd be given an extraordinarily beautiful image, of the nobility of what their love could be"

"When you wake up to the Divine Consciousness within you and your divine identity, you wake up simultaneously to the Divine Consciousness appearing as all other beings. And this is not poetry and this is not a feeling, this is a direct experience of the divine light living in and as all other beings. And until this realization is firm in you, you do not know who or where you are."

"What a recovery of the wisdom of the Mother brings to all of us is the knowledge of inseparable connection with the entire creation and the wise, active love that is born from that knowledge."

Andrew Harvey, gay mystic

LIBERATION

Gay people are confused. Tired of being told we are unnatural, sinners, mentally ill or less valid than heterosexuals, when we do get the courage to come out it can feel like the struggle is over and it is understandable if we just want to party and have lots of sex. We are breaking out of a dark closet, emerging from a long tunnel of persecution. There are voices telling us we are more than we think we are, that our love can be noble and spiritual and enlightening, that we have a calling to bring peace and tolerance to the world, but they are up against the din of voices screaming against us. No wonder we shut off, make partying our religion, and some of us end up lost in drug crazed states of disconnection.

The cause of Gay Liberation has achieved much in some parts of the world, but it can only change the picture globally, change the world's understanding of us, if it goes all the way and we recognise that gay liberation is human liberation. Surely Gay liberation is about all people being free to be who they are, to answer the call of their own soul, and being free to love whom they choose. The rainbow flag represents that all races, all genders, all sexualities are parts of one humanity who are united in our need to love and be loved. This is the profoundly spiritual message gay, plus lesbian, bi and trans people bring to the world, as we challenge religious types to live up to their holy ideals of love and compassion and to extinguish the cruel flames of intolerant laws and attitudes coming from a time when heterosexual males were setting themselves up as the leaders of society, when they were dismantling the power long held by females, especially their spiritual power, and so attacking all traces of feminine energy in men too, in so doing changing the ancient perception of the earth as our Mother into a resource to be plundered.

Coming Out is not the end of the journey. We come out because we hear a deep call from the soul to be our true selves. The thing is to keep listening to the soul and learn that life's crises, such as as an HIV diagnosis, are calls to do just that. We need to complete the journey. Sexuality is only part of who we are. It's important that we celebrate and explore our sexuality, and indeed we can use it to fuel our spiritual liberation too. Sexual liberation – political liberation – social and spiritual liberation must all go together. That way we will see the Wholeness, we will be the Wholeness and the Wholeness will be us.

Shokti

ALL ACTS OF LOVE AND PLEASURE ARE HER RITUALS

The Goddess told me.......

that we are her children
the celebrants of life
gay girls, faerie boys, andro kids
lovers of beauty, pleasure and joy
lovers of lovers of love
born to give and receive
and to make – love

she told me in love there is a secret
that people haven't worked out yet
a mystery leading to the unveiling
of the multi layered reality
our eyes have barely begun to see
or is that in our obsessions
we have forgotten how to look

she told me she is waiting
until the darkest hour
but her love is always there
for those who turn to her

she is waiting for the dance to start
for the veils to lift
and reveal her throne
dancing faeries attend her
and angels do her bidding
she will come with comfort for the kind at heart

fury for the corrupt, abusive and greedy
and rage against those who persecute her gentle kids

shekhinah, shakti, maid, mother, crone
she never wanted her children to cope alone
but the men of war would have their day
until the turning of the way
she stepped back, hid as the virgin
but in heaven she is still queen

sniff the spirit
whisper
divine mother is near
we don't have to know it all
to know ourselves
leaves journey as do stars
we are forever in the dance

those who awaken to the mother
awaken the divine child within themselves

divine mother is here
and she is calling to the queer
calling us to drop the fear
know the transformation's near
lift up our hearts and be sincere
our eternal mother is here

all acts of love and pleasure are her rituals

"Let us bless the tribe of all tribes that brought us into the world, bless the people through whose sacred bodies other people come. Let us bless all the scouting peoples, whose ancient and forgotten wisdom is being remembered in this time. And let us bless each other and ourselves. It is for this that our ancestors worked, that we ourselves worked in other lives – so that all of humanity, and we the tribe of men who love men, can step into this new era, the time of love on Earth."

Andrew Ramer, **Two Flutes Playing**

postscript

THE GLITTER BALL

the glitter ball
sits in the middle of the disco, its many tiny mirrors each
reflecting the light
as we dance under the ball, hands in the air, we feel our unity,
the power of our tribe
the disco takes us beyond our separate bodies
we feel our spirits become one
the glitter ball reflects the light onto us
one ball… many mirrors… creating patterns of light
reflecting us
one humanity… many faces… creating patterns of life

the glitter ball IS THE HOLY SYMBOL of the global queer
spirit …
in the 70s disco music brought a taste of heaven to earth
in the 80s house music opened the multidimensional gateways
in the 90s rave brought love and transcendence to the masses
in the naughties the light was lost in a swarm of drugs and
consumerism
that separated and confused instead of united
anaesthetics replacing psychedelics and euphoric helpers

the glitter ball symbolises that from one source of light comes
many reflections
and as we dance we know we are those reflections
not separate from each other, except in body and mind
no wonder it is the greatest joy to bring those bodies together

unite them in dance, in touch, in sex
finding again our oneness
and if we learn to empty our minds, find the infinite field of
peace
we can merge in the mindspace too, in a psychic psychedelic
symphony
nature, spirit and humankind

on dance floors the world over, the glitter ball says....
we are one light dancing, loving, playing
that is why we are here, that is why we are queer
the rest of humanity does not get who we are
and even though we too have fallen for their lies
we are the dancing spirit, and through our dance, through our
love, through our sex
we open the gates of consciousness
but, obsessed with the material world, rejecting the religious
past
humanity has largely forgotten that other dimensions exist
time to reclaim our roles as the healers, witches and shamans
let's open the gates, let the love and light of the Great Spirit
through
and shock the discoknickers off the world.

Www.queerspirit.net
www.rainbowmessengerblog.wordpress.com
www.shokti.wordpress.com

all words and drawings by Shokti unless otherwise stated

#0120 - 131217 - C0 - 210/148/0 - PB - DID2065145